Pre-Algebra

by
Bob Olenych

SCHOLASTIC
PROFESSIONAL BOOKS
New York • Toronto • London • Auckland • Sydney
Mexico City • New Delhi • Hong Kong • Buenos Aires

DEDICATION

To all of the students who enjoyed participating in my math classes.

Cover design by Josué Castilleja
Cover illustration by Mike Moran
Interior design by Melinda Belter
Interior illustrations by Steve Cox

ISBN 0-439-43110–7

Printed in the U.S.A.

1 2 3 4 5 6 7 8 9 10 40 10 09 08 07 06 05 04 03

Table of Contents

Introduction

A GLANCE AT PRE-ALGEBRA

Students who have been exposed to pre-algebraic concepts, who enjoy what's been taught, and who can transfer their skills to other concepts, will make the transition to algebra without too many difficulties. To help my students gain fluency and accuracy, I often create practice puzzles and activities that they really enjoy. The problems and puzzles in this book motivate my students to sharpen their order of operations skill as well as the skills necessary to work with integers, equations, variables, square roots, exponents, and even cryptarithms. They also help students to develop the strategies and confidence they'll need to tackle bigger mathematics challenges they'll encounter in school and beyond.

WHAT YOU'LL FIND IN THIS BOOK

This book offers a collection of pre-algebraic activities addressing a broad range of skills and abilities. The puzzles are arranged according to skill, from easy to difficult, and they cover a wide range of activities. You can match the needs of your students and target a specific skill by checking the skill description listed in the table of contents.

One skill I have always enjoyed teaching to my students is order of operations. By playing an order of operations card game, students learn a variety of strategies that they can apply and even transfer to other problems. Initially my students may have been somewhat "intimidated" by the numbers that were randomly selected, but they all rose to the challenge and learned how to write mathematically correct number sentences that may have included one, two, or even all three sets of brackets. To have students regularly ask to have an order of operations challenge as a homework assignment definitely speaks to the success and fun of this game. Try it, and I'm positive both you and the class will enjoy it.

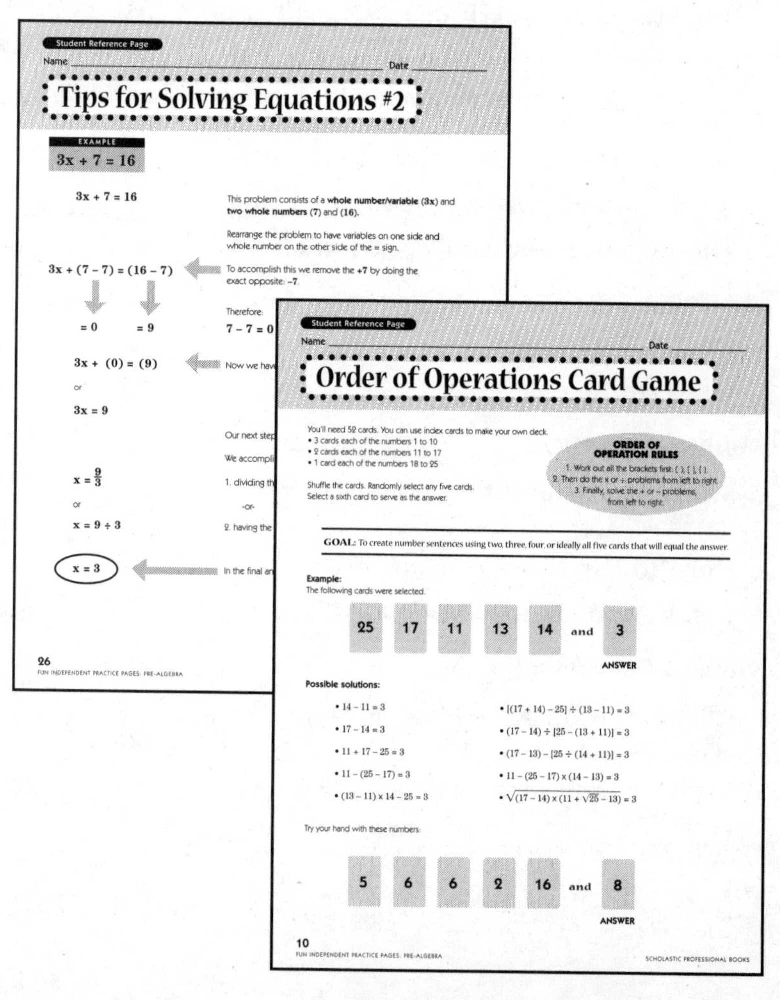

Student Reference Page

Name ____________ Date ______

Tips for Solving Equations #2

EXAMPLE
3x + 7 = 16

3x + 7 = 16 — This problem consists of a **whole number/variable (3x)** and **two whole numbers (7)** and **(16)**.

Rearrange the problem to have variables on one side and whole number on the other side of the = sign.

3x + (7 – 7) = (16 – 7) — To accomplish this we remove the **+7** by doing the exact opposite: **–7**.

= 0 **= 9** — Therefore: **7 – 7 = 0**

3x + (0) = (9) — Now we hav

or

3x = 9

Our next step

We accompli

x = 9/3 — 1. dividing th

or — -or-

x = 9 ÷ 3 — 2. having the

x = 3 — In the final an

26
FUN INDEPENDENT PRACTICE PAGES: PRE-ALGEBRA

Student Reference Page

Name ____________ Date ______

Order of Operations Card Game

You'll need 52 cards. You can use index cards to make your own deck.
- 3 cards each of the numbers 1 to 10
- 2 cards each of the numbers 11 to 17
- 1 card each of the numbers 18 to 25

Shuffle the cards. Randomly select any five cards.
Select a sixth card to serve as the answer.

ORDER OF OPERATION RULES
1. Work out all the brackets first: ( ), [ ], { }.
2. Then do the x or ÷ problems from left to right.
3. Finally, solve the + or – problems, from left to right.

GOAL: To create number sentences using two, three, four, or ideally all five cards that will equal the answer.

Example:
The following cards were selected.

25 17 11 13 14 and 3
ANSWER

Possible solutions:
- 14 – 11 = 3
- 17 – 14 = 3
- 11 + 17 – 25 = 3
- 11 – (25 – 17) = 3
- (13 – 11) x 14 – 25 = 3
- [(17 + 14) – 25] ÷ (13 – 11) = 3
- (17 – 14) ÷ [25 – (13 + 11)] = 3
- (17 – 13) – [25 ÷ (14 + 11)] = 3
- 11 – (25 – 17) x (14 – 13) = 3
- $\sqrt{(17 - 14) \times (11 + \sqrt{25} - 13)} = 3$

Try your hand with these numbers:

5 6 6 2 16 and 8
ANSWER

10
FUN INDEPENDENT PRACTICE PAGES: PRE-ALGEBRA
SCHOLASTIC PROFESSIONAL BOOKS

HOW TO USE THIS BOOK

Be sure to use these puzzles in a way that best suits the needs of your class. You may find it helpful to assign certain pages as practice work to follow a lesson, as review work, or as homework. You also may want to have students work on different pages depending on the skills each student needs to practice. The beauty of these activities is that, because the right answers solve a riddle or puzzle, almost all of the activities are self-correcting. Whether they are solving a riddle, breaking a code, or filling in a number puzzle, students are encouraged to check each problem so that they can finish the puzzle successfully. If a student's answer does not correspond with one of the answers provided, or it creates a glitch in the riddle, students realize that they've made an error and will double-check their work to arrive at the correct solution.

CONNECTIONS TO THE MATH STANDARDS

Most of the puzzles in this book target the NCTM 2000 objectives listed under the Number and Operations standard. These objectives include understanding ways to represent numbers, determining meanings of operations and how they relate to one another, and computing with fluency and accuracy. This book is packed with word problems that require students to use the operations of addition, subtraction, multiplication and division. Many of the problems deal with time, area, perimeter, and weight, and there is also practice involving the standardized test format.

I'm confident that your students, like mine, will enjoy this collection of word problems and reap the benefits of practicing these essential skills.

Bob Olenych

Name ______________________________ Date ______________

Donut Business

Complete the two sets of problems by inserting the correct signs of operations. The signs are to the right of each problem and must be used in the order they are given. Write the word below the signs on the answer line that corresponds to the question number to solve the following riddle.

Why did the baker stop making donuts?

SET 1

1.	8 □ 4 □ 5 = 7	× − SHE	+ − HE	− × AHMED
2.	8 □ $\sqrt{4}$ □ 3 = 7	+ × IS	− + ISN'T	÷ + WAS
3.	8 □ 4 □ 3 = 7	+ ÷ EVENTUALLY	÷ + STEADILY	− + GRADUALLY
4.	8 □ $\sqrt{4}$ □ 3 = 7	+ − GETTING	+ ÷ BECOMING	− + APPEARING
5.	4 □ 3 □ 5 = 7	× + SUPER	× − VERY	+ − EASILY

SET 2

6.	2 □ 7 □ 6 = 3	× − EXHAUSTED	+ − TIRED	+ + OVERWORKED
7.	7 □ 6 □ 2 = 3	+ − WITH	− + OF	− − OFF
8.	7 □ (10 □ 6) = 3	− − THE	+ − A	+ + AN
9.	6 □ $\sqrt{2 \; □ \; 7}$ = 3	+ + WHOLE	− × BAKERY	− + HOLE
10.	7 □ $\sqrt{10 \; □ \; 6}$ = 3	+ − THING	− + BUSINESS	− − OCCUPATION

1. ____________ 2. ____________ 3. ____________ 4. ____________ 5. ____________

6. ____________ 7. ____________ 8. ____________ 9. ____________ 10. ____________ .

Name ________________________________ Date ______________

Tic-Tac-Toe

Complete all the number sentences. If your answer is an even number, give that space an **X**, but if your answer is an odd number, give it an **O**. Any three **X**s or **O**s in a straight line wins.

$5 \times 2 + [(6 + 2) \div 8] =$	$(5 \times 6) - 8 \times (2 \div 2) =$	$2 \times 8 - [2 - (6 - 5)] =$
$8 \times 2 - [(6 - 5) \times 2] =$	$(8 + 6 + 5) + (2 \div 2) =$	$\sqrt{2 + 2} \times 8 + (6 - 5) =$
$(5 + 2 + 2) \times (8 - 6) =$	$(5 \times 6) - 8 + (2 \div 2) =$	$8 + 6 + 5 + \sqrt{2 \times 2} =$

Name ______________________________ Date ______________

The Zookeeper's Observation

Complete these problems by inserting the correct signs of operation. The signs are to the right of each problem and must be used in the order they are given. Write the word below the signs on the answer line that corresponds to the question number to solve the following riddle.

What observation did the zookeeper make about the young kangaroo?

1. 2 – [(6 ☐ 5) – (8 ☐ 2)] = 1	– + GEORGE	+ – SHE	X – KATIE	+ + HE
2. (6 + 5 ☐ 8 ☐ 2) x 2 = 2	+ – LEARNED	– X WITNESSED	– – DISCOVERED	– + OBSERVED
3. 2 ☐ [(6 + 5) ☐ (8 + 2)] = 3	+ – THAT	– + WHAT	+ X WHICH	X – WHEN
4. 8 ☐ [(6 – 5) x (2 ☐ 2)] = 4	– + IT	X + KANGAROOS	– – ANIMALS	+ – MARSUPIALS
5. (2 ☐ 2) x 8 ☐ 6 + 5 = 5	– – COULDN'T	+ X SHOULDN'T	– X CANNOT	X – WOULDN'T
6. (2 – 2) ☐ 8 x 5 ☐ 6 = 6	– + LEAP	X + HOP	+ – STRIDE	+ X JUMP
7. (5 + 2) x [(6 ☐ 2) ☐ 8] = 7	÷ + BUT	+ – UNLESS	– X SINCE	+ ÷ AND
8. (5 ☐ 2) ☐ [(6 + 2) ÷ 8] = 8	+ ÷ WAS	– + SEEMS	+ + IS	X – APPEARS
9. $\sqrt{(8-6)\ ☐\ 2}$ ☐ 2 + 5 = 9	+ – TOTALLY	X X UTTERLY	– X USUALLY	X – OFTEN
10. 5 ☐ 2 x [(6 + 2) ☐ 8] = 10	+ ÷ HOPELESS	– X USELESS	X ÷ HOPLESS	– – CARELESS

1. ______________ 2. ______________ 3. ______________ 4. ______________ 5. ______________

6. ______________ 7. ______________ 8. ______________ 9. ______________ 10. ______________ .

Name ______________________________ Date ____________

The Dentist's Job

Solve the following number sentences, then arrange your answers from LEAST to GREATEST in the boxes below. Then write the word from each problem above the matching answers. When you have completed all the problems, you will decode the following riddle.

How did the dentist describe her work to her friends?

1. $6 \times 4 \div 3 + (6 + 5)$ = ______ = **GRIND**
2. $(8 \times 3 + 11) \div (5 + 2)$ = ______ = **SAID**
3. $[(6 + 2) \times 2] \div (7 \div 7)$ = ______ = **OLD**
4. $\sqrt{6 \times 8 \div 3} \times 2 + 5$ = ______ = **SAME**
5. $[(24 - 17) + (7 \times 2)] \div 3$ = ______ = **IT'S**
6. $\sqrt{(5 + 3) \times 8} \div 2 \times 6$ = ______ = **DAY**
7. $20 - \{4 \times [9 - (8 - 3)]\}$ = ______ = **SHE**
8. $5 + [(5 \times 4) - (\sqrt{25} \times 3)]$ = ______ = **THE**
9. $\{12 - [15 - (2 \times 6)]\} \times 5$ = ______ = **DAY**
10. $(\sqrt{36} - \sqrt{25}) \times (8 + 7) \times 2$ = ______ = **AFTER**

Least

.

Greatest

Name ______________________ Date __________

Order of Operations Card Game

You'll need 52 cards. You can use index cards to make your own deck.

- 3 cards each of the numbers 1 to 10
- 2 cards each of the numbers 11 to 17
- 1 card each of the numbers 18 to 25

Shuffle the cards. Randomly select any five cards. Select a sixth card to serve as the answer.

ORDER OF OPERATION RULES

1. Work out all the brackets first: ( ), [ ], { }.
2. Then do the x or ÷ problems from left to right.
3. Finally, solve the + or – problems, from left to right.

GOAL: To create number sentences using two, three, four, or ideally all five cards that will equal the answer.

Example:

The following cards were selected.

25 17 11 13 14 and 3

ANSWER

Possible solutions:

- $14 - 11 = 3$
- $17 - 14 = 3$
- $11 + 17 - 25 = 3$
- $11 - (25 - 17) = 3$
- $(13 - 11) \times 14 - 25 = 3$
- $[(17 + 14) - 25] \div (13 - 11) = 3$
- $(17 - 14) \div [25 - (13 + 11)] = 3$
- $(17 - 13) - [25 \div (14 + 11)] = 3$
- $11 - (25 - 17) \times (14 - 13) = 3$
- $\sqrt{(17 - 14) \times (11 + \sqrt{25} - 13)} = 3$

Try your hand with these numbers:

5 6 6 2 16 and 8

ANSWER

Name ______________________________ Date ____________

Riddle Time

Solve the following problems and find your answer in the code boxes below. To solve the riddle, write the letter from each problem in the code box with the matching answer. If the same answer appears in more than one box, fill in each one with the same letter.

What happens to people who make sponges?

$(.7 \times .3) + \text{(M)} = 4.39$ **M** =

$(.5 \times \text{(B)}) - 1.4 = .85$ **B** =

$(.03 \times .3) + 3.13 = \text{(W)}$ **W** =

$(\text{(H)} \times .7) - .31 = .18$ **H** =

$(.001 \times 53) + \text{(N)} = 6.453$ **N** =

$(7.5 \times \text{(T)}) - .043 = .032$ **T** =

$(7 \times .8) + 4.3 = \text{(A)}$ **A** =

$(.7 \times 15) - \text{(Y)} = 3.6$ **Y** =

$(\text{(C)} \times .13) + .48 = .519$ **C** =

$(.6 \times .9) - .09 = \text{(D)}$ **D** =

$(\text{(E)} \times .08) + 6.2 = 6.2064$ **E** =

$(.09 \times .8) - .07 = \text{(R)}$ **R** =

$(4 \times \text{(K)}) + 6.7 = 11.5$ **K** =

$(24 \times .05) - \text{(I)} = 1.13$ **I** =

$(.3 \times \text{(O)}) + 4.003 = 4.993$ **O** =

$(\text{(S)} \times .06) - .013 = .041$ **S** =

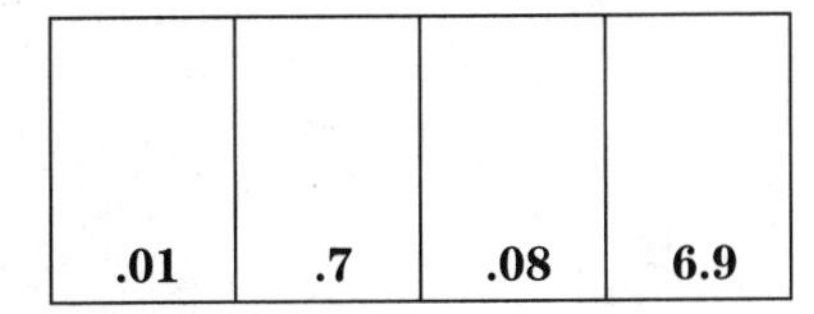

.01	.7	.08	6.9

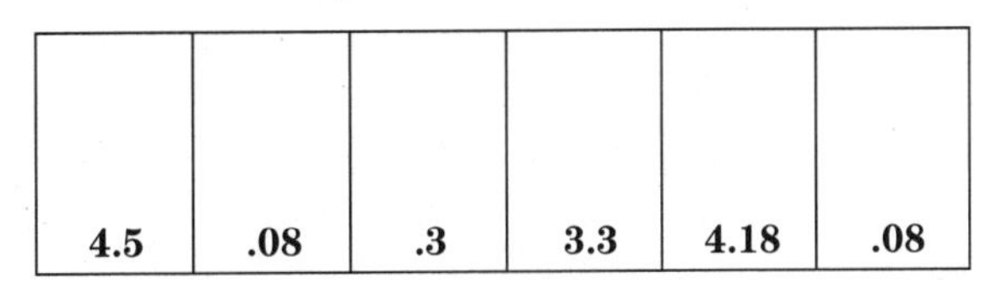

4.5	.08	.3	3.3	4.18	.08

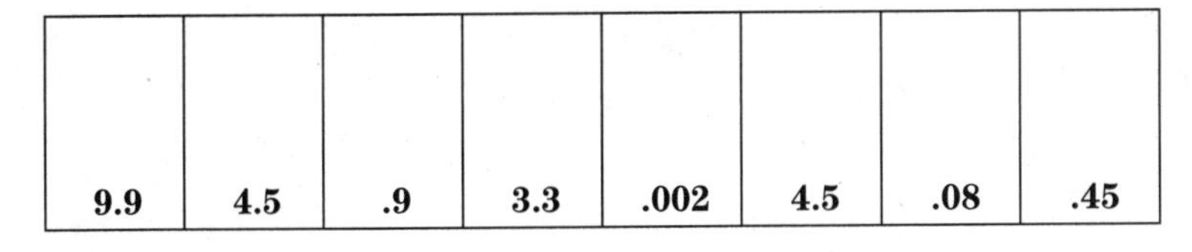

9.9	4.5	.9	3.3	.002	4.5	.08	.45

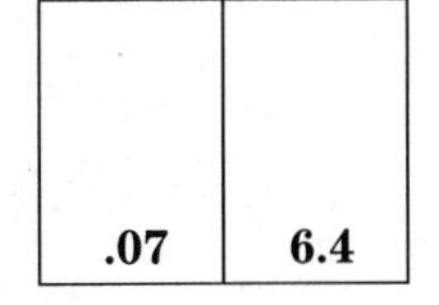

.07	6.4

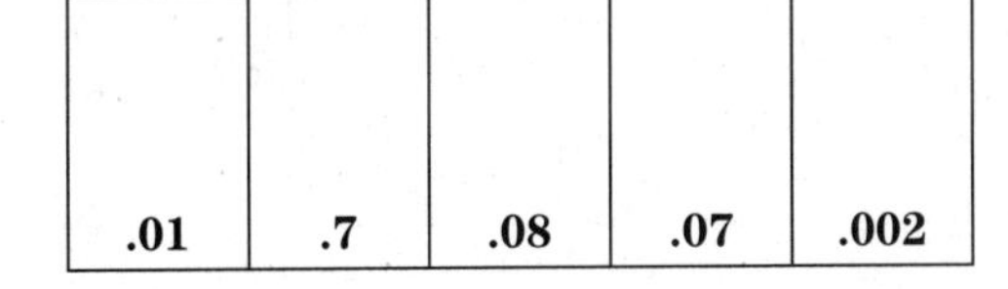

.01	.7	.08	.07	.002

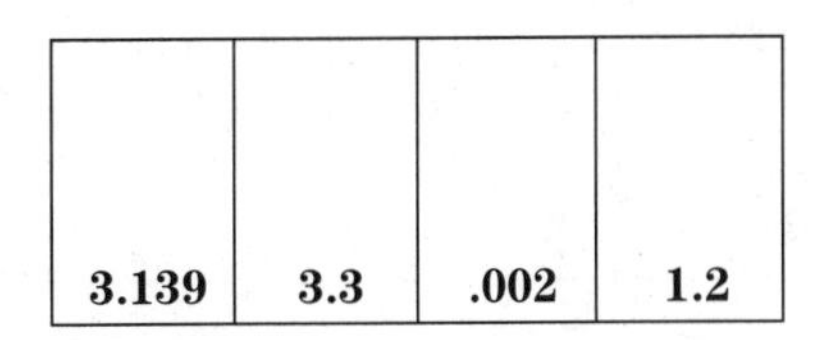

3.139	3.3	.002	1.2

.

Name ______________________________ Date ____________

Match It #1

Solve the problems below, then locate each correct answer in the column on the right. Use a ruler or a straightedge to draw a line from the question to the answer (dot to dot). Your line will pass through a number and a letter. The number tells you where to write your letter in the code boxes to answer the riddle below.

What did the nurse say to the anxious father after his little boy swallowed some coins?

$(8.4 - 4.9) + \square = 8$ •	• 9.1
$(3\frac{1}{8} + 4\frac{4}{8}) - \square = 7\frac{1}{2}$ •	• 8
$\square - (2.1 + 2.5) = 4\frac{1}{2}$ •	• $5\frac{5}{12}$
$3\frac{5}{6} - \square + 2\frac{3}{6} = 6$ •	• $\frac{1}{8}$
$\square + 4.6 + .8 = 13.4$ •	• $1\frac{4}{4}$
$6\frac{1}{2} + 2\frac{2}{4} - \square = 7$ •	• 4.5
$2\frac{2}{12} + \square + 3\frac{2}{12} = 10\frac{3}{4}$ •	• $3\frac{2}{3}$
$4.2 + 2.1 + \square = 8\frac{7}{10}$ •	• $\frac{2}{6}$
$\square + (2\frac{2}{3} + 5\frac{1}{3}) = 11\frac{2}{3}$ •	• $6\frac{4}{5}$
$13.13 - 8.03 - \square = 2.08$ •	• 3.02
$7\frac{3}{5} - 2\frac{1}{5} + \square = 12\frac{1}{5}$ •	• 2.4

7 O 4 G 10 A R 5 9 T C 8 S 1 3 E N 2 Y 11 H 6

1	2	3	4	3

’

5

6	7

8	2	9	6	10	3

11	3	1

.

Name ______________________________ Date ____________

Equal Values

Solve the problems in both sets of boxes. Then match each answer in the top boxes to an equivalent answer in the bottom boxes. Also identify whether the commutative **C**, the associative **A**, or the identity **I** properties of addition or multiplication were used by circling the **C**, **A**, or **I**. Discover the answer to the following riddle by writing each word from the top set of boxes in the boxes underneath with the matching answer.

What did people say about the girl who couldn't decide if she wanted to be a pilot?

2 + (9 + 8) + 3 = **MAKE**	8 + 5 + 6 + 2 = **STILL**	27 + 0 = **IN**	4 x 3 x (2 x 6) = **GIRL**
12 x 1 = **UP**	2 x 3 x 4 x 5 = **THE**	(4 x 5) x 2 = **UP**	3 x 9 x 2 = **YOUNG**
4 x 3 x 2 x 2 = **CAN'T**	9 + 9 + 6 + 5 = **MIND**	(12 + 9) + 9 = **SHE**	2 x (8 x 2) x 10 = **HER**
6 x (10 x 5) = **AIR**	0 + 82 = **IS**	3 + 9 + 8 + 4 + 7 = **SIMPLY**	(5 x 3) x 2 x 2 = **THE**

2 x 3 x (5 x 2) = C A I	2 x 3 x 9 = C A I	(6 x 4) x 2 x 3 = C A I	4 + 7 + 8 + 9 + 3 = C A I
2 x 4 x 2 x 3 = C A I	2 + (9 + 8 + 3) = C A I	1 x 12 = C A I	(10 x 8) x 2 x 2 = C A I
5 + 9 + 6 + 9 = C A I	(9 + 9) + 12 = C A I	82 + 0 = C A I	5 + 8 + 2 + 6 = C A I
(2 x 5) x 4 = C A I	0 + 27 = C A I	5 x 3 x 2 x 4 = C A I	(6 x 5) x 10 = C A I

Name ______________________ Date __________

Match It #2

Solve the problems below, then locate each correct answer with an underlined number in the opposite column. Use a ruler or a straightedge to draw a line from the answer to the underlined number (dot to dot). Your line will pass through a number and a letter. The number tells you where to write your letter in the code boxes to answer the riddle below.

Where can camels purchase milk?

29 + 6 = ☐ •	• 27 + 9 = ☐
19 x 5 = ☐ •	• 222 ÷ 6 = ☐
36 – 9 = ☐ •	• 12 x 8 = ☐
92 ÷ 4 = ☐ •	• 35 – 6 = ☐
37 x 6 = ☐ •	• 78 + 9 = ☐
48 + 3 = ☐ •	• 120 ÷ 8 = ☐
87 – 9 = ☐ •	• 95 ÷ 5 = ☐
96 ÷ 8 = ☐ •	• 23 x 4 = ☐
44 – 5 = ☐ •	• 39 + 5 = ☐
15 x 8 = ☐ •	• 51 – 3 = ☐

M 9 R 4 8 I R 2 6 A D E 5 7 Y D 1 10 O 3

1	2	3	4	5	6	7	8	9	10

Name ______________________________ Date ____________

Reciprocal Tic-Tac-Toe

Solve the two problems in each section. If both answers in that section are the same (for example, both answers are whole numbers, or both are proper fractions), give that section an **X**. If the answers are different (for example, one is a proper fraction, one is a whole number, or one is an integer), give it an **O**. Any three **X**s or **O**s in a straight line wins.

Find the reciprocal of:

A. $\frac{3}{30}$ **B.** $\frac{1}{8}$

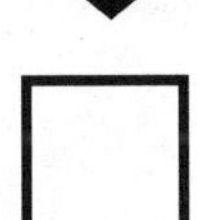

Find the reciprocal of:

A. $1\frac{1}{4}$ **B.** $\frac{5}{9}$

Find the reciprocal of:

A. $\frac{5}{8}$ **B.** $\frac{3}{4}$

Find the reciprocal of:

A. $-\frac{2}{3}$ **B.** $\frac{5}{6}$

Find the reciprocal of:

A. $\frac{1}{5}$ **B.** $\frac{2}{6}$

Find the reciprocal of:

A. $-\frac{4}{9}$ **B.** $\frac{1}{2}$

Find the reciprocal of:

A. $1\frac{2}{3}$ **B.** $2\frac{1}{8}$

Find the reciprocal of:

A. $\frac{2}{12}$ **B.** $\frac{2}{9}$

Find the reciprocal of:

A. $\frac{5}{14}$ **B.** $\frac{4}{8}$

Name ______________________________ Date ______________

Let's Play Bingo

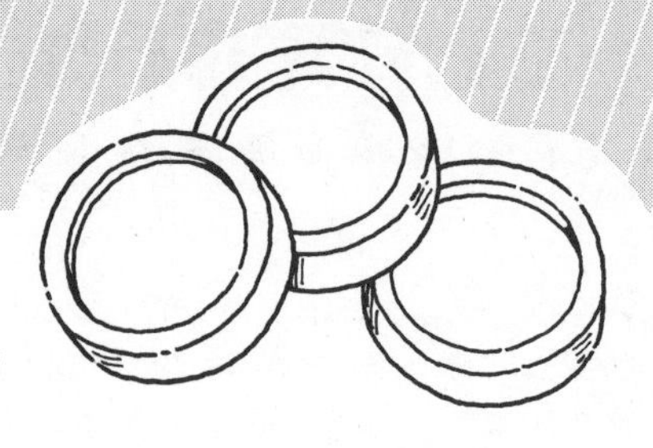

Solve the problems below by using the distributive property to simplify each expression. Locate your answers in the bingo grid. Circle the answers you find in the grid. Any five answers in a line horizontally, vertically, or diagonally is a **BINGO**.

1. $5(x + 2) =$

2. $y(8 - 2) + 6 =$

3. $9n + 7 - 4n =$

4. $7(p + 3) - 6 =$

5. $4x + 6x - 3x =$

6. $5(k + 4) =$

7. $n(5 - 3) + 4 =$

8. $8p + 6p + 7 =$

9. $2y + 7y + 8 =$

10. $4x + 3x - 7 =$

11. $3(k + 8) + 5k =$

12. $k(8 - 4) + 5 =$

13. $3(y + 4) + 4 (y + 4) =$

14. $3(n + 7) + 2n =$

15. $p(6 + 4) + 8 =$

BINGO

4k + 5	2n + 4	8x – 6	14p + 7	7n – 7
7y + 28	12p – 3	3x + 5	3k – 9	8k + 24
4n + 5	6k + 13	5n + 21	5x + 10	8y – 5
7x	5y + 15	6p	5k + 20	7x – 7
9y + 8	7p + 15	5n + 7	10p + 8	6y + 6

Name ______________________________ Date ____________

Lumberjack Special

Determine the answer for each shaded box by completing the relation rule in the six tables. The value of **x** is provided in the column on the left. Each answer indicates where the letter should go in the code boxes below. Complete the activity to solve the following riddle.

What specialty food was served at the Lumberjack Café?

x	$5x - 3$	
5	22	
	37	M
6	27	
4		E
2	7	

x	x^2	
	9	P
4		H
7	49	
8	64	
9		V

x	$x^2 + 4$	
5		D
2	8	
6	40	
	104	A
7	53	

x	$4x + 2$	
4	18	
	50	I
9		C
3	14	
	62	R

x	$7x - 5$	
13		N
8	51	
	9	S
9	58	
7		T

x	$x^2 - 7$	
4	9	
	42	Y
3	2	
8		L
	114	O

44	16	17	7

2	17	15	81	17	29

8	10	12	86	57	7

38	16	11	3	2

.

Name ______________________________ Date ____________

Question and Answer

Solve these problems by completing the relation rule using the values of **x** and **y** which are provided in the two left columns. Then write each answer from least to greatest in the 19 boxes below. Write the word found in the answer boxes in the corresponding boxes below to reveal a question and an answer. (Please ignore the five answers which were given as examples.)

x	y	$x + 3y$	$3x - y$	$x^2 - 2$	$y^2 + 4$
4	5	MOST	DO	THEIR	BE
7	2	RATE	19	HARD	MOST
9	4	FIND	THAT	DEEP-ENDS	SWIMMERS
3	6	21	HOW	7	OR
6	7	CAN	PEOPLE	EASY	IT
9	3	SWIMMING	SWIMMING	79	13

QUESTION:

?

Least

ANSWER:

			–		

.

Greatest

Name ______________________________ Date ____________

The Amazing Waiter

In each of the problems, you are given the value of **x** and the answer. Determine which of the four choices was used to arrive at the answer. Write the word found with your choice on the answer line that corresponds to the question number to solve the following riddle.

What was the tennis-playing waiter's talent?

1. **If x = 5**

$2x + 10$ **WE**	x^3 **SHE**
$5x$ **HE**	$3x - 5$ **THE**

= 10

2. **If x = 6**

$4x - 7$ **EASILY**	x^2 **FINALLY**
$6x$ **SURELY**	$7x - 9$ **WAITER**

= 33

3. **If x = 9**

$4x$ **ISN'T**	x^2 **WASN'T**
$3x + 3$ **WAS**	$2x - 1$ **IS**

= 30

4. **If x = 7**

$4x + 10$ **ONE**	$42x$ **AN**
$12x - 9$ **THE**	x^2 **A**

= 49

5. **If x = 8**

$4x - 7$ **SLOW**	$6x$ **FAST**
x^2 **TALL**	$7x - 9$ **TALENTED**

= 47

6. **If x = 4**

$2x - 1$ **DIVER**	$x^2 - 15$ **SERVER**
x^2 **BAKER**	$4x$ **RUNNER**

= 1

________ ________ ________ ________ ________ ________ .

Question 1 **Question 2** **Question 3** **Question 4** **Question 5** **Question 6**

Name ______________________ Date __________

Hidden Answer

Read the ordered pairs (for example: 1, 5) listed in the code boxes below. Find the letter of the alphabet that names each point given. Write the correct letter in the box above the ordered pair to reveal the answer to the following question.

What comment did the parent make about having children?

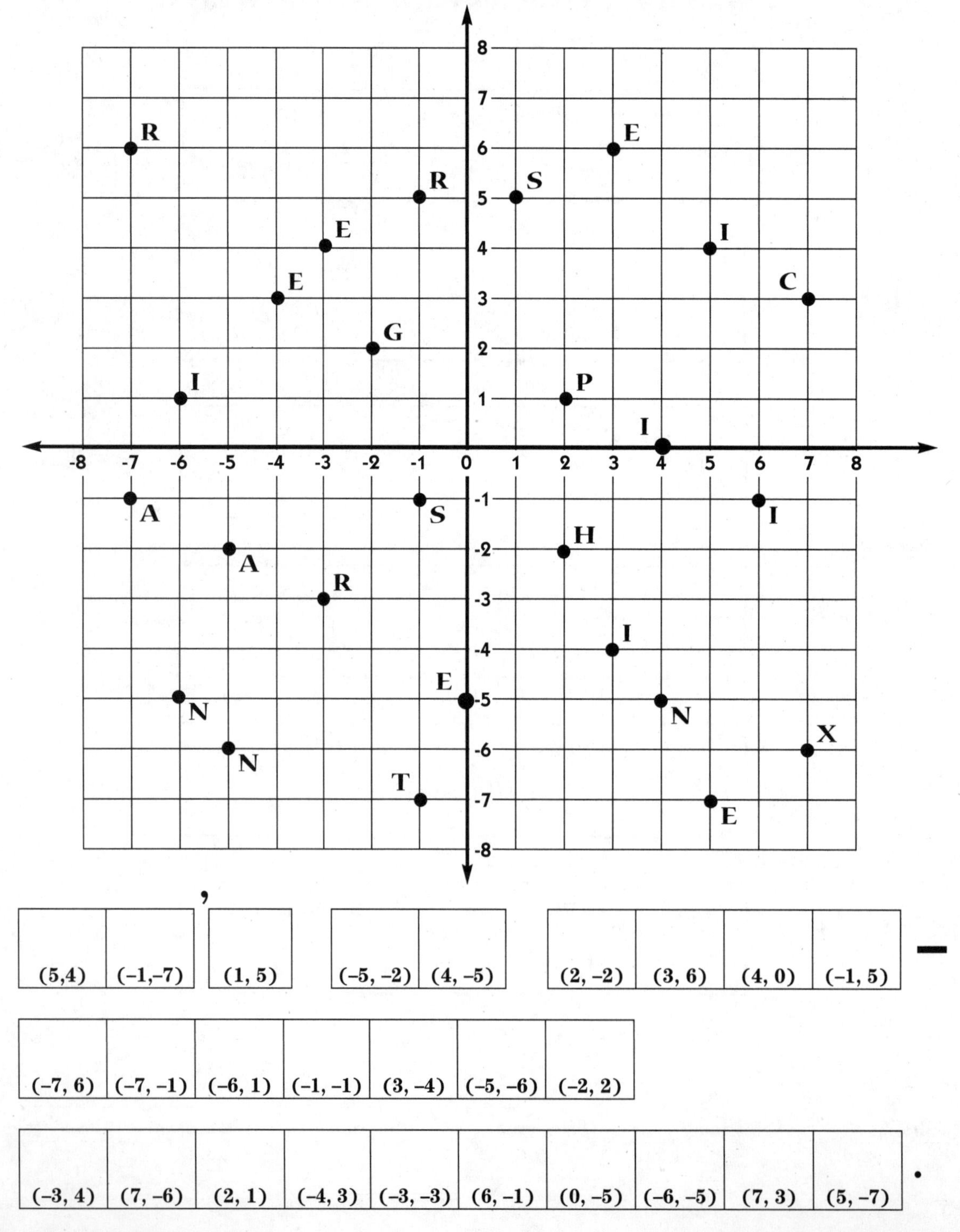

(5,4)	(−1,−7)	’ (1, 5)		(−5, −2)	(4, −5)		(2, −2)	(3, 6)	(4, 0)	(−1, 5)	–

(−7, 6)	(−7, −1)	(−6, 1)	(−1, −1)	(3, −4)	(−5, −6)	(−2, 2)

(−3, 4)	(7, −6)	(2, 1)	(−4, 3)	(−3, −3)	(6, −1)	(0, −5)	(−6, −5)	(7, 3)	(5, −7)	.

Name ______________________________ Date ____________

The Wedding

Determine the ordered pair that names each of the 24 numbered points in the coordinate plane. Find the ordered pairs listed below and write the correct number next to each pair. Then write each letter on the code line that corresponds to the number under the line to reveal the answer to the following riddle.

What did the people say after the TV repairman got married?

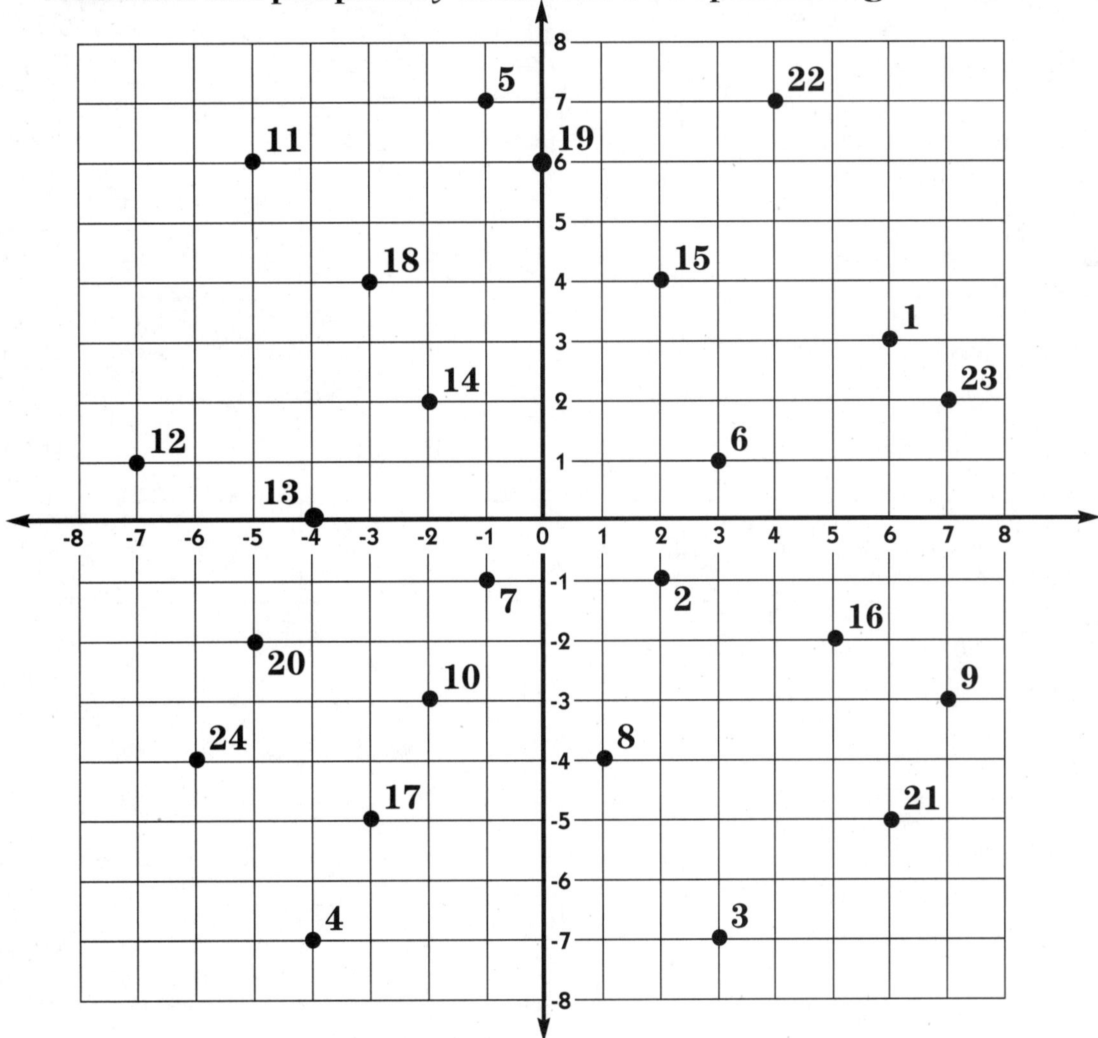

(3, 1) = _____ = **C**	(1, –4) = _____ = **P**	(–2, –3) = _____ = **I**	(5, –2) = _____ = **E**	(7, 2) = _____ = **N**	(–1, 7) = _____ = **E**
(–5, –2) = _____ = **L**	(4, 7) = _____ = **E**	(6, 3) = _____ = **T**	(–6, –4) = _____ = **T**	(3, –7) = _____ = **E**	(–1, –1) = _____ = **E**
(7, –3) = _____ = **T**	(–4, –7) = _____ = **R**	(6, –5) = _____ = **L**	(2, 4) = _____ = **S**	(–5, 6) = _____ = **O**	(0, 6) = _____ = **E**
(–3, 4) = _____ = **C**	(–7, 1) = _____ = **N**	(–2, 2) = _____ = **A**	(–4, 0) = _____ = **W**	(2, –1) = _____ = **H**	(–3, –5) = _____ = **X**

___ ___ ___   ___ ___ ___ ___ ___ ___ ___ ___ ___
1 2 3   4 5 6 7 8 9 10 11 12

___ ___ ___   ___ ___ ___ ___ ___ ___ ___ ___ ___.
13 14 15   16 17 18 19 20 21 22 23 24

Name ______________________________ Date ____________

Movie Star Doctor

Solve the following problems by writing a mathematical expression in the correct column. Then solve each expression using the value of **x** provided. To solve the following riddle, write the word from each problem on the code line with the matching answer.

Why do lots of movie stars go to the cosmetic surgeon?

	Mathematical Expression		Answer	
1. Twice a number, decreased by 5		if **x** = 5		= **TO**
2. The product of a number and 4, increased by 2		if **x** = 7		= **KNOWS**
3. A number increased by 5⁄4		if **x** = 3⁄4		= **DROOPY**
4. The sum of a number and 8		if **x** = 10		= **RAISE**
5. A number increased by 15		if **x** = 4		= **SURGEON**
6. Eight times a number divided by 4		if **x** = 3		= **FEW**
7. A number decreased by 7		if **x** = 10		= **THE**
8. One-half of a number		if **x** = 8		= **A**
9. Seven times a number divided by 2		if **x** = 6		= **HOW**
10. Twice a number increased by ½		if **x** = ⅓		= **EYEBROWS**

______ **3** ______ **19** ______ **30** ______ **21** ______ **5**

______ **18** ______ **4** ______ **6** ______ **2** ______ **7⁄6 or 1 1⁄6** .

Name ____ Date ______________

Hard to Swallow

If **x = 6** and **y = 5**, find the answer represented by each of the following expressions. To solve the riddle, write the word from each problem in the code box with the matching answer.

What happened to the lady who swallowed a spoon?

$4x + 4y =$	= **OF**
$6(x + y) + 3y =$	= **QUICKLY**
$3x + 3y + 4y + 5x =$	= **STIR**
$7x - 2y + 15 =$	= **THAT**
$9x - 4y + 2x =$	= **WITHIN**
$2(x + y) + 4(x + y) =$	= **SHE**

$5(x + y) =$	= **MINUTES**
$7x + 4y + 2x =$	= **SHE**
$6x + (5x - 3y) =$	= **A**
$5x + 3y - 2(x - y) =$	= **LEARNED**
$5y + 7y + 8y =$	= **COULDN'T**
$8x + 2y + 6y - 4x =$	= **MATTER**

46	51	64	44	55	66

81	43	47	74	100	83

Name ______________________________ Date ______________

Party Animals

Find the answers represented by each of the following expressions by using the values provided for the variables in the shaded sections. To solve the riddle, write the word from each problem on the code line with the matching answer.

What do bees do after building a hive?

k = 4 and **m** = 3	**x** = 5 and **y** = 4
PARTY = $2k - 2m$ = ______	HUGE = $xy - x - y$ = ______
a = 4 and **b** = 6	**p** = 3 and **q** = 7
HIVE = $(a + b)^2$ = ______	AT = $p^3 + 2q$ = ______
g = 2 and **h** = 3	**m** = 8 and **n** = 9
A = $g^2 h^2 - g^2$ = ______	SWARMING = $3m + 4n - 15$ = ______
r = 3 and **s** = 10	**j** = 3 and **k** = 5
THE = $5r + s^2 + 3s$ = ______	THEY = $36 - 2j - 2k$ = ______
v = 6 and **w** = 4	**d** = 6 and **f** = 5
HOUSE = $5(v + w) + 2w$ = ______	HAVE = $16 + d + f^2$ = ______

______ 20 ______ 47 ______ 32 ______ 11 ______ 58 –

______ 45 ______ 2 ______ 41 ______ 145 ______ 100 .

Name ______________________________ Date ____________

Tips for Solving Equations #1

EXAMPLE

$7m = 49$

$7m = 49$

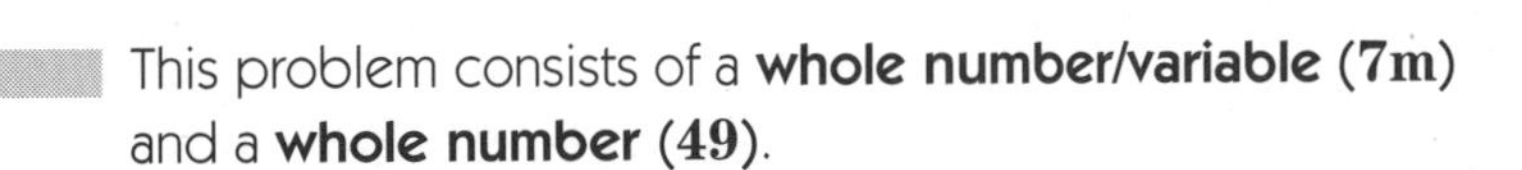

This problem consists of a **whole number/variable** ($7m$) and a **whole number** (49).

$7 \times m = 49$

When we are asked to **SOLVE**, that means the m must stand alone without the whole number **7**.

We accomplish this by:

$m = \frac{49}{7}$

1. dividing the whole number **7** into the whole number **49**

or

-or-

$m = 49 \div 7$

2. having the **49** divided by **7**.

$m = 7$

EXAMPLE

$\frac{1}{3}s = \frac{4}{7}$

$\frac{1}{3}s = \frac{4}{7}$

This problem consists of a **fraction/variable** ($\frac{1}{3}s$) and a **fraction** ($\frac{4}{7}$).

$\frac{1}{3} \times s = \frac{4}{7}$

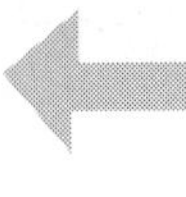

When we are asked to **SOLVE**, that means the s must stand alone without the fraction ($\frac{1}{3}$).

We accomplish this by:

$s = \dfrac{\frac{4}{7}}{\frac{1}{3}}$

1. dividing the fraction $\frac{1}{3}$ into the fraction $\frac{4}{7}$

or

-or-

$s = \frac{4}{7} \div \frac{1}{3}$

2. $\frac{4}{7}$ divided by $\frac{1}{3}$.

$s = \frac{4}{7} \times \frac{3}{1}$

(With fractions, remember to reverse the second fraction and multiply.)

$s = \frac{12}{7}$ or $s = 1\frac{5}{7}$

Name ____________________ Date __________

Tips for Solving Equations #2

EXAMPLE

$3x + 7 = 16$

$3x + 7 = 16$

This problem consists of a **whole number/variable** (**3x**) and **two whole numbers** (**7**) and (**16**).

Rearrange the problem to have variables on one side and whole number on the other side of the = sign.

$3x + (7 - 7) = (16 - 7)$

To accomplish this we remove the **+7** by doing the exact opposite: **–7**.

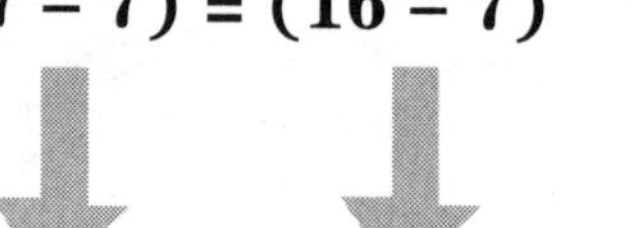

$= 0$ $= 9$

Therefore:

$7 - 7 = 0$ and $16 - 7 = 9$

$3x + (0) = (9)$

Now we have this equation.

or

$3x = 9$

Our next step is to have the **x** stand alone.

We accomplish this by:

$x = \frac{9}{3}$

1. dividing the **3** into the **9**

-or-

or

$x = 9 \div 3$

2. having the **9** divided by **3**.

$x = 3$

In the final answer, the variable (**x**) must stand alone.

Name ______________________________ Date ____________

Take Your Pick

Solve the following equations and find each of your answers under the code lines below. (Remember to express all fractions in their simplest terms.) To solve the riddle, write the word from each problem on the line with the matching answer.

What is the difference between a pitchfork and a toothpick?

KNOW	DO	DIFFERENCE
$2k = 15$ $k =$	$7n = 49$ $n =$	$12q = 156$ $q =$
TEETH	**HAD**	**NOT**
$8b = 64$ $b =$	$42d = 378$ $d =$	$6p = 32$ $p =$
YOUR	**IF**	**PICK**
$\frac{1}{3}g = 7$ $g =$	$5x = 125$ $x =$	$\frac{1}{2}w = 6$ $w =$
BETTER	**THE**	**YOU**
$7f = \frac{3}{4}$ $f =$	$\frac{2}{3}m = 4$ $m =$	$4j = 56$ $j =$
YOU	**REALLY**	**NOT**
$6y = 43$ $y =$	$15s = 225$ $s =$	$5z = \frac{1}{2}$ $z =$

________	________	________
25	**14**	**15**
________	________	________
7	**$\frac{1}{10}$**	**$7\frac{1}{2}$**
________	________	________
6	**13**	**$7\frac{1}{6}$**
________	________	________
9	**$\frac{3}{28}$**	**$5\frac{1}{3}$**
________	________	________ .
12	**21**	**8**

Name ____ Date ______________

Shapely Math

21x	3x	10x
2x	9x	15x
8x	18x	7x

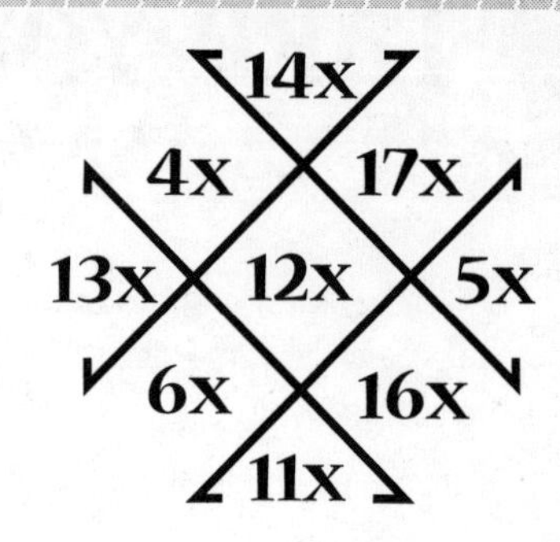

Study the shapes in equations 1 to 6. Each shape has only one match in the number grids at right. Use the shapes to fill in the missing numbers in the equations. Solve each number sentence and find your answer in the Answer Box below. (Remember to express all fractions in their simplest form.)

1. (+) – (+) = 21 **x** =

2. (+) – (+) = 21 **x** =

3. (–) – (–) = 17 **x**=

4. (–) + (–) = 50 **x** =

5. (+) – (–) = 13 **x** =

6. (–) + (–) = 75 **x** =

ANSWER BOX

2 1/6	5	3 1/8	3
8 1/2	4 1/6	5 2/3	9 1/3
2 1/3	7	6 3/4	6

Hint:
There are 6 answers in the Answer Box that you will not use.

Name ______________________________ Date ____________

Cross Them Out

Solve all the equations below, remembering to express all answers in lowest terms. Locate and cross out each of the correct answers in the grid. (Answers run horizontally, left to right.) When you have finished, 33 boxes will remain. Write the remaining letters in order from left to right and top to bottom to reveal the answer to the following riddle. The first problem has been done for you.

What did people say about the boy who resembled his father, the sculptor?

$\frac{1}{2}y = \frac{3}{4}$	$y = 1\frac{1}{2}$	$\frac{3}{7}z = \frac{1}{2}$	$z =$	$\frac{2}{3}x = \frac{3}{6}$	$x =$
$\frac{1}{6}n = \frac{1}{2}$	$n =$	$\frac{1}{4}d = \frac{3}{5}$	$d =$	$\frac{3}{5}t = \frac{1}{3}$	$t =$
$\frac{3}{4}f = \frac{2}{3}$	$f =$	$\frac{2}{3}p = \frac{4}{5}$	$p =$	$\frac{3}{6}b = \frac{1}{4}$	$b =$
$\frac{4}{5}s = \frac{2}{3}$	$s =$	$\frac{1}{2}k = \frac{6}{9}$	$k =$	$\frac{2}{3}m = \frac{4}{9}$	$m =$

$\frac{3}{4}$ A	5 T	$\frac{8}{9}$ S	2 H	$\frac{4}{5}$ E	2 B	$\frac{2}{5}$ L	6 L	$\frac{1}{3}$ I	$\frac{7}{8}$ T
8 T	$\frac{1}{6}$ L	1 O	$\frac{1}{2}$ S	4 E	$\frac{1}{4}$ L	8 A	$\frac{2}{5}$ D	$\frac{1}{2}$ S	7 I
5 S	$\frac{5}{9}$ T	6 A	$\frac{2}{5}$ C	1 K	$\frac{1}{5}$ S	4 H	$\frac{7}{9}$ I	1 S	$\frac{1}{3}$ S
8 P	$\frac{4}{7}$ O	2 F	2 F	7 T	$\frac{2}{3}$ O	8 H	$\frac{11}{12}$ E	4 O	4 L
3 R	6 D	$\frac{1}{9}$ B	$\frac{5}{6}$ R	8 L	$\frac{7}{8}$ O	7 C	$\frac{3}{7}$ K	1 E	$\frac{1}{6}$ S

___ ___ ___   ___ ___ ___ ___ ___ ___   ___ ___ ___

___ ___   ___   ___ ___ ___ ___   ___ ___ ___

___ ___ ___   ___ ___ ___   ___ ___ ___ ___ ___ .

Name ______________________________ Date ______________

Happiness is . . . ?

Solve the following equations and find your answer in the code boxes below. To solve the riddle, write the word from each problem in the code box with the matching answer.

When are horses happiest while eating?

$3x + 2x - 5 = 5$	$x =$	= **THEIR**	$7m - 3m + 4 = 16$	$m =$	= **DON'T**
$4p + 6p - 2p = 17$	$p =$	= **A**	$3k + 2k - 5 = 30$	$k =$	= **IN**
$3c + c + 3 = 24$	$c =$	= **REALLY**	$8n - 2n + 6 = 36$	$n =$	= **WHEN**
$5b + 3b - 7 = 41$	$b =$	= **THEY**	$2z + 3z + 5 = 45$	$z =$	= **THEY**
$6s - 4s - 12 = 6$	$s =$	= **THEIR**	$2t + 5t - 4 = 26$	$t =$	= **ENJOY**
$3r + 4r - 7 = 11$	$r =$	= **OATS**	$7g - 4g + 4 = 9$	$g =$	= **HAVE**
$8d - 6d + 3 = 8$	$d =$	= **MOUTHS**	$2f + 4f + 9 = 29$	$f =$	= **BIT**

6	**$5\frac{1}{4}$**	**$4\frac{2}{7}$**	**2**	**$2\frac{4}{7}$**	**5**	**8**

3	**$1\frac{2}{3}$**	**$2\frac{1}{8}$**	**$3\frac{1}{3}$**	**7**	**9**	**$2\frac{1}{2}$**

Name ______________________________ Date ______________

Ancient Gatherings

To solve this riddle, complete the problems below. The number line travels left to right with intersections one unit apart. You are required to move either left or right from the starting point indicated in the first column of the chart. When you have finished filling in the chart, the number in the Numeral at Destination column tells you where to write the letter from the Start column on the lines below. The first problem has been done for you.

What did cave dwellers do when they got together?

Y	F	C	S	B	T	L	E	O	R	M	G	D	E	H	P	U
–8	–7	–6	–5	–4	–3	–2	–1	0	1	2	3	4	5	6	7	8

START	DIRECTION	LETTER AT DESTINATION	NUMERAL AT DESTINATION
O	move 6 units left	C	-6
S	move 9 units right		
R	move 9 units left		
T	move 5 units right		
B	move 3 units right		
H	move 8 units left		
Y	move 5 units right		
D	move 11 units left		
U	move 8 units left		
M	move 4 units right		
E	move 6 units right		
L	move 3 units right		
F	move 3 units right		
C	move 13 units right		
E	move 10 units left		

__ __ __ __   __ O __ __ __ __ __   __ __ __ __ __ .

2 -2 5 -3   -4 -6 -8 6 -5 -7   7 1 0 -1 4

Name ______________________________ Date ____________

Cats on Vacation

To solve this riddle, complete the problems that accompany each number line, moving in the direction indicated. The number lines travel east and west of zero, with intersections one mile apart. Each time you land on a destination, circle the letter above it. When you have completed all the problems, print the circled letters in the answer spaces below, starting from the top line and moving from left to right.

Where do cats like to go on vacation?

WEST

EAST

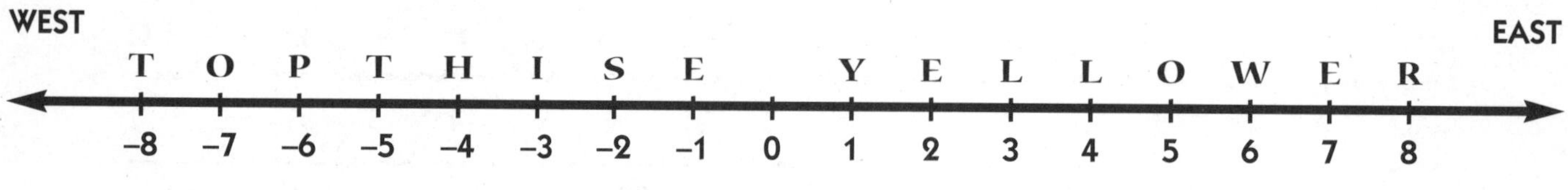

4 miles west of 7
10 miles west of 6

9 miles east of –4
2 miles east of –7

6 miles east of –5
4 miles west of 3

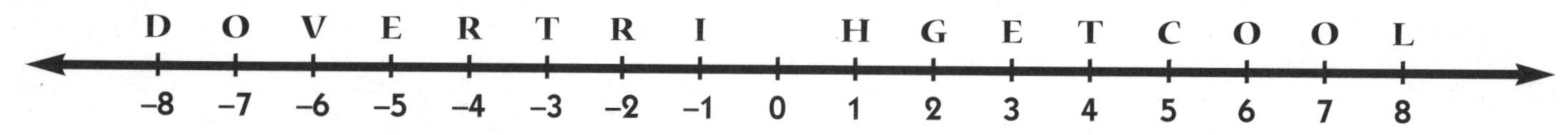

12 miles east of –7
12 miles west of 6

7 miles west of 4
5 miles east of –2

7 miles west of 2
8 miles east of –7

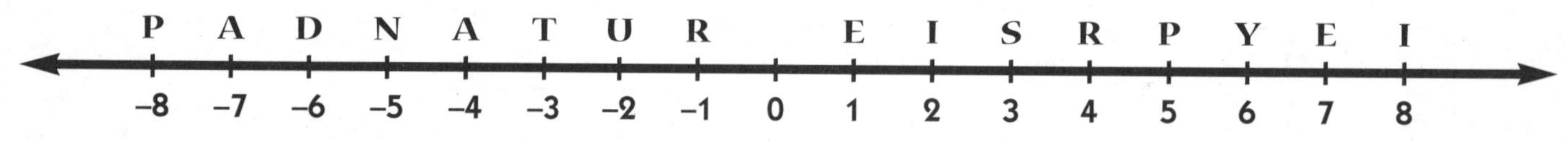

4 miles west of 0
8 miles east of –2

9 miles west of 2
9 miles west of 4

7 miles east of –3
11 miles east of –3

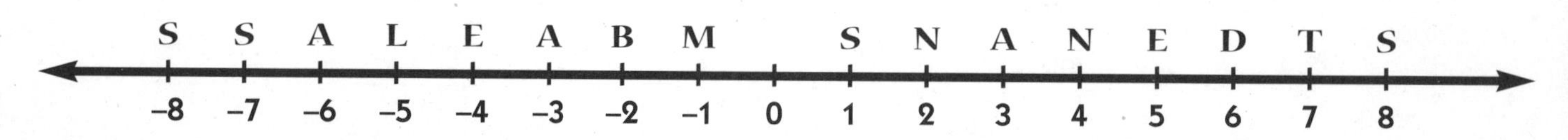

6 miles west of –1
12 miles west of 7

10 miles east of –4
11 miles east of –3

9 miles east of –5
6 miles west of 3

____ ____ ____ ____   ____ ____ ____ ____   ____ ____ ____

____ ____ ____ ____ ____ ____   ____ ____ ____ ____ ____ ____ ____ .

Name ____________________________________ Date ______________

The Lucky Janitor

Each of the boxes below consists of two problems. Solve the problem on the left and write the answer in the box below the problem. Do the same for the problem on the right side. Then add the two answers together and record it in the oval. To solve the riddle, write the word from each problem in the code box with the matching answer.

Hint: To subtract an integer, add its opposite.

How did the janitor meet his wife?

$^{+}20 + ^{+}5 + ^{-}15 =$ ☐ + ☐ $= ^{+}20 + ^{-}10 + ^{-}6$ ◯ = **OFF**	$^{+}60 - ^{+}40 - ^{-}32 =$ ☐ + ☐ $^{+}13 + ^{-}13 + ^{-}13 =$ ◯ = **A**
$^{+}60 + ^{-}20 + ^{-}40 =$ ☐ + ☐ $^{+}9 + ^{-}11 - ^{-}7 =$ ◯ = **WITH**	$^{-}42 + ^{-}12 + ^{+}20 =$ ☐ + ☐ $^{-}30 - ^{+}22 - ^{-}10 =$ ◯ = **SWEPT**
$^{-}24 - ^{+}12 - ^{+}6 =$ ☐ + ☐ $^{+}16 + ^{-}14 + ^{-}20 =$ ◯ = **HER**	$^{+}9 + ^{-}6 + ^{-}11 =$ ☐ + ☐ $^{-}18 - ^{+}25 + ^{-}7 =$ ◯ = **BROOM**
$^{-}15 + ^{-}9 + ^{+}10 =$ ☐ + ☐ $^{+}20 + ^{+}14 + ^{-}8 =$ ◯ = **FEET**	$^{+}21 - ^{-}9 - ^{+}5 =$ ☐ + ☐ $^{-}30 - ^{+}15 - ^{-}5 =$ ◯ = **HER**

He:

$^{-}76$	$^{-}15$	$^{+}14$	$^{-}60$	$^{+}12$	$^{+}5$	$^{+}39$	$^{-}58$

.

Name ______________________________ Date ____________

Let's Play Ball

In the problems below, solve all the number sentences enclosed within the square root signs, and write your answers in the spaces provided. Then arrange all of the answers from least to greatest in the column on the right side of the page. Write the word found next to the answer in the corresponding boxes to reveal the answer to the riddle below.

Why did the toy poodle like to play baseball?

$\sqrt{3 \times 12 + (3 \times 5 - 2)} =$ ____ = **HOME**

$\sqrt{28 \div 7 \times 4} + \sqrt{20 \times 5 - (24 - 5)} =$ ____ = **GET**

$\sqrt{4 \times 9 + 12 + (7 \times 3 - 5)} =$ ____ = **PLATE**

$\sqrt{25} + \sqrt{35 - (8 + 2)} + \sqrt{4} =$ ____ = **TO**

$\sqrt{7 \times 5 - (12 - 2)} - \sqrt{(16 + 16) \div 8} =$ ____ = **HE**

$\sqrt{72 \div 8} \times \sqrt{36 \div 4} =$ ____ = **HE**

$\sqrt{24 - 16 + 1} \times \sqrt{40 \div 5 - 4} =$ ____ = **TO**

$\sqrt{36 - (2 \times 10)} + \sqrt{49} + \sqrt{18 \div 2} =$ ____ = **WALKED**

$\sqrt{7 + 3 + (8 \times 2) - 1} =$ ____ = **UP**

$\sqrt{4 \times 8 + (4 \times 4 \times 2)} \div \sqrt{13 - 9} =$ ____ = **GOT**

$\sqrt{(8 \times 12) - (5 \times 3)} + \sqrt{14 \times 2 \div 7} =$ ____ = **SURE**

$\sqrt{36} - \sqrt{16} =$ ____ = **WHENEVER**

$\sqrt{(8 \div 4 \times 15 - 5) \times 4} =$ ____ = **WAS**

LEAST

	=
	=
	=
	=
	=
	=
	=
	=
	=
	=
	=
	=
	=

GREATEST

Name ______________________________ Date ____________

The Noisy Twins

Solve all of the number sentences below, remembering to pay close attention to the numbers expressed as exponents (e.g., $2^3 = 2 \times 2 \times 2 = 8$). With a ruler or a straightedge, connect all of the answers (dot to dot) from the greatest to the least. Then copy the words beneath the answers in the spaces below to answer the following riddle.

What did the man say about the pair of loud twins?

$2^5 + 7^2 + 9^2 =$ ☐ **HE**

$10^3 - (10^2 \times 8) \div 4 =$ ☐ **AS**

$12^2 + 4^2 - 7 =$ ☐ **TO**

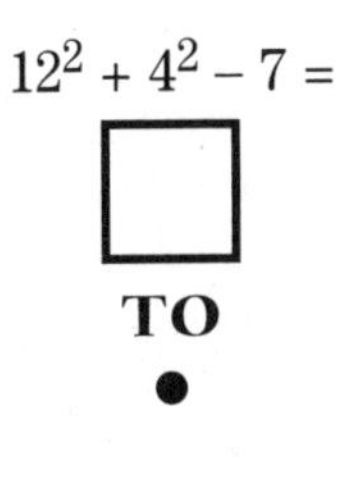

$(3^3 + 98) \div 5^2 =$ ☐ **STEREO**

$7^2 \times 4 - 6^2 =$ ☐ **REFERRED**

$6^2 + 7^2 - 9^2 =$ ☐ **SPEAKERS**

$24 + 7^2 + 3^3 =$ ☐ **BOYS**

$2^4 \times 5 + 8^2 =$ ☐ **THE**

$5^3 - 4^2 + 3 =$ ☐ **TWIN**

$10^2 + 5 + 3^2 =$ ☐ **IDENTICAL**

GREATEST

LEAST

Name ______________________________ Date ____________

The Lost Timepiece

To solve this riddle, complete each of these problems by inserting **a number written as an exponent or as a square root.** Locate your answer in the code boxes and write the letter from the matching problem above it. If the answer appears in more than one box, fill in each one with the same letter.

What happened to the beautiful lady who lost her watch?

$(36 \div 3) + [17 + (6 \times 7)] - E = 62$	**E** =
$A - [(2 \times 12) + (7 \times 5 + 6)] = 16$	**A** =
$T + [(12 \times 10) - (7 \times 9 + 1) - (7 \times 8)] = 11$	**T**=
$[(5 \times 4 + 6) + (9 \times 8 + 2)] - (S \times 10) = 0$	**S** =
$61 - (8 \times 5) + U = 57$	**U** =
$5 \times 6 + (7 \times 8) - Y = 81$	**Y** =
$L - [(12 \times 5) - 24 + (7 \times 4)] = 61$	**L** =
$25 + (9 \times 12) - (4 \times 4 \times 2) - C = 89$	**C** =
$34 - (5 \times 4) + (6 \times 7) - M = 24$	**M** =
$(15 \times 2 + 30) - (27 \div 3 \times 2) - H = 34$	**H** =
$(12 \times 12) - (5 \times 5 \times 5) + (56 \div 2) + B = 111$	**B** =
$I + [(81 \div 9) + (5 \times 2 + 2)] = 48$	**I** =

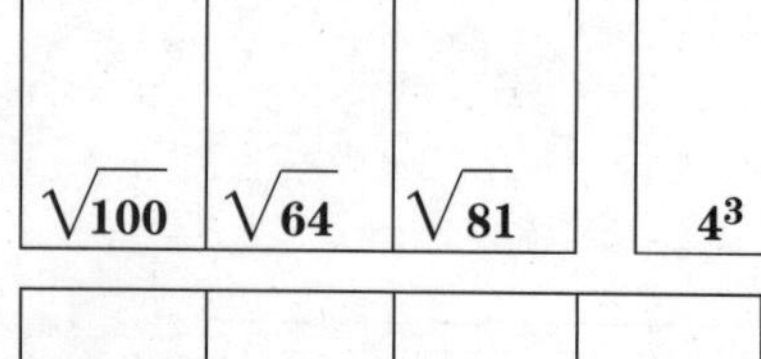
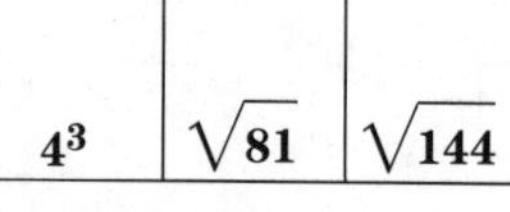
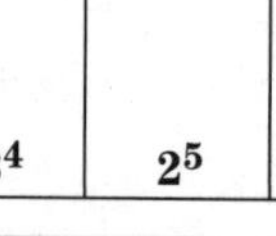
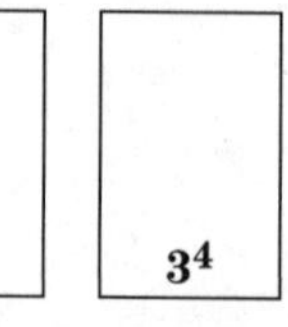

$\sqrt{100}$	$\sqrt{64}$	$\sqrt{81}$	4^3	$\sqrt{81}$	$\sqrt{144}$	3^4	2^5	$\sqrt{81}$	3^4	

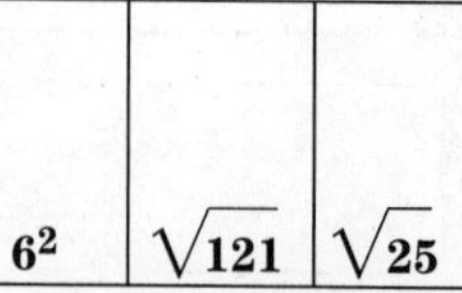

$\sqrt{121}$	3^3	2^5	$\sqrt{81}$	5^3	$\sqrt{81}$	$\sqrt{100}$	$\sqrt{100}$	4^3	$\sqrt{81}$	3^4	6^2	$\sqrt{121}$	$\sqrt{25}$

.

Name ______________________________ Date ____________

The Young Artist

Solve the following inequalities to determine which mathematical statement is **TRUE** or **FALSE**. Circle the correct answer. The letter and number below the answer indicate where the letter should be written on the code lines to answer this riddle.

Why couldn't the young artist draw a cube?

Statement	TRUE	FALSE	Statement	TRUE	FALSE
$9 + 3 < 13$	M 7	B 3	$11 - 4 > 6$	O 5	R 7
$(18 - 11) - (2 \times 2) \neq 3$	E 11	L 14	$(25 \div 5) \div 5 > 4 \times 9 \div 6$	C 13	N 9
$8.5 + 6.5 > (3 \times 4) + (9 \div 3)$	N 2	E 3	$14 + 7 > 25$	W 1	A 6
$24 - (7 \times 2) > 2^3$	A 11	C 5	$5.005 > 5.05$	I 4	D 1
$2\frac{1}{9} + 3\frac{4}{9} \neq 5\frac{1}{3} + \frac{2}{9}$	T 9	O 15	$(24 \div 3) + 16 > 7 \times 6 \div 2$	E 8	R 14
$26 - (3 \times 2 + 2) < 64 \div 8 + 1$	O 2	K 17	$(21 + 24) \div 9 \neq \sqrt{25}$	D 12	T 4
$(9 \times 8 + 8) \div 10 > 24 \div 4 + 2$	A 15	U 2	$3.5 \times 6 > 19.4 + 3.6$	A 8	L 12
$10\frac{7}{10} \neq \frac{2}{5} + 10\frac{1}{5} + \frac{1}{10}$	O 16	B 13	$3^2 + 2^4 = 5^2$	C 16	G 10
$3.03 < 3\frac{30}{100}$	T 10	S 17			

The artist just couldn't— ___ ___ ___ ___ ___ ___
1 2 3 4 5 6

___ ___ ___ ___ ___ ___ ___ ___ ___ ___ ___ .
7 8 9 10 11 12 13 14 15 16 17

Name ______________________ Date ____________

The Clockmakers' Cat

Determine the solution set for each inequality and write your answer in the space between the sets of brackets below. Write the word from each problem on the line with the matching answer to solve the riddle.

What did the clockmakers find out about their cat?

$4x < 24$ { } **TO**	$m > 4$ { } **THEY**	$5k < 35$ { } **TOOK**
$3b > 18$ { } **HAD**	$10p < 20$ { } **WHEN**	$m > 3$ and $m < 9$ { } **VETERINARIAN'S**
$9y < 36$ { } **IT**	$x + 7 < 12$ { } **TICKS**	$3q + 1 > 7$ { } **THEY**
$7s + 6 > 27$ { } **THE**	$3k + 3 < 30$ { } **IT**	$5d - 4 > 1$ { } **DISCOVERED**

______ **{0, 1 }** ______ **{3, 4, 5, 6 . . .}** ______ **{0, 1, 2, 3, 4, 5, 6}** ______ **{0, 1, 2, 3, 4, 5, 6, 7, 8}**

______ **{0, 1, 2, 3, 4, 5}** ______ **{4, 5, 6, 7, 8 . . .}** ______ **{4, 5, 6, 7, 8}** ______ **{5, 6, 7, 8 . . .}**

______ **{2, 3, 4, 5 . . .}** ______ **{0, 1, 2, 3}** ______ **{7, 8, 9, 10 . . .}** ______ **{0, 1, 2, 3, 4}** .

Name ______________________________ Date ____________

The Unhappy Tree

Complete the pattern in each problem by selecting the correct ordered pair from the three answers provided. The letter and number below each answer indicate where the letter should be written in the code boxes to answer the following riddle.

Which evergreen tree always seems unhappy?

(60, 36), (50, 25), (40, 16), (■ , ■)

(30, 11)	(30, 9)	(30, 7)
A 6	**P 5**	**W 0**

(67, 70), (72, 65), (77, 60), (■ , ■)

(81, 55)	(82, 50)	(82, 55)
M 0	**E 5**	**L 1**

(2, 4), (6, 36), (18, 324), (■ , ■)

(54, 2592)	(54, 2916)	(54, 2268)
O 3	**E 9**	**W 4**

(12, 10), (15, 12), (18, 14), (■ , ■)

(21, 18)	(20, 16)	(21, 16)
L 3	**M 8**	**U 7**

(9, 81), (10, 100), (11, 121), (■ , ■)

(12, 132)	(12, 148)	(12, 144)
S 7	**L 2**	**C 8**

(54, 100), (45, 120), (36, 140), (■ , ■)

(26, 150)	(27, 160)	(27, 150)
G 4	**U 2**	**H 8**

(81, 3), (64, 9), (49, 27), (■ , ■)

(25, 81)	(36, 72)	(36, 81)
I 9	**P 3**	**R 6**

(23, 5), (22, 15), (20, 35), (■ , ■)

(17, 65)	(16, 75)	(16, 65)
S 4	**N 6**	**E 5**

(128, 4), (64, 7), (32, 10), (■ , ■)

(18, 13)	(16, 12)	(16, 13)
L 4	**R 7**	**B 0**

(3, 33), (5, 55), (7, 77), (■ , ■)

(9, 89)	(9, 99)	(8, 88)
L 6	**E 3**	**A 2**

The | 0 | 1 | 2 | 3 | | 4 | 5 | 6 | 7 | 8 | 9 | .

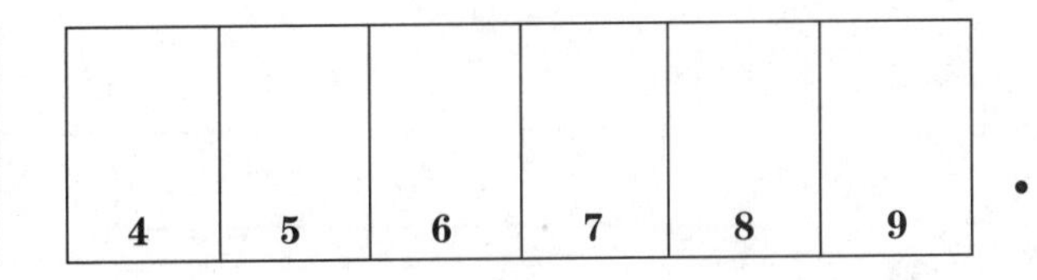

Name ______________________________ Date ______________

The Curious Boy

Study the three samples in each of the seven problems to determine the pattern. Continue the pattern by solving **two** more equations. Four possible answers are in boxes below each problem. Once you have chosen your answers, write the word beneath the answer on the code line that matches the number in ( ).

Why did the little boy throw the butter off the balcony?

IF 9 x 4 = 36 99 x 4 = 396 999 x 4 = 3996		WHAT IS: 99999 x 4 = __________ AND 999999 x 4 = __________	
39996	3999996	39999996	399996
SUN (14)	**CURIOUS (5)**	**HOT (13)**	**THE (12)**

IF 10 x 10 = 100 20 x 20 = 400 30 x 30 = 900		WHAT IS 70 x 70 = __________ AND 90 x 90 = __________	
8100	2500	4900	3600
WAS (3)	**THE (1)**	**WANTED (9)**	**IT (8)**

IF 6 x 7 = 42 66 x 67 = 4422 666 x 667 = 444222		WHAT IS 6666 x 6667 = __________ AND 666666 x 666667 = __________	
44444422222	444444222222	44442222	4444422222
IN (11)	**SEE (11)**	**BUTTER (13)**	**TO (6)**

IF 100 ÷ 11 = 9.09090 90 ÷ 11 = 8.18181 80 ÷ 11 = 7.27272		WHAT IS 70 ÷ 11 = __________ AND 40 ÷ 11 = __________	
6.36363	5.45454	4.84848	3.63636
AND (6)	**REALLY (4)**	**MELT (10)**	**BOY (2)**

(continued on next page)

Name ______________________ Date ____________

The Curious Boy (continued)

IF 11 x 11 = 121 111 x 111 = 12321 1111 x 1111 = 1234321		WHAT IS 11111 x 11111 = ________ AND 1111111 x 1111111 = ________	
12345654321	1234567654321	123454321	123456787654321
THE (12)	**TO (10)**	**SIMPLY (8)**	**LAD (2)**

IF 9 x 11 = 99 19 x 21 = 399 29 x 31 = 899		WHAT IS 39 x 41 = ________ AND 59 x 61 = ________	
1499	1599	3499	3599
QUICKLY (9)	**THE (1)**	**HOPING (5)**	**FLY (14)**

IF 11 x 22 = 242 11 x 222 = 2442 11 x 2222 = 24442		WHAT IS 11 x 22222 = ________ AND 11 x 2222222 = ________	
24444442	2444442	244444442	244442
HE (7)	**WAS (3)**	**WATCH (7)**	**VERY (4)**

______ 1 ______ 2 ______ 3 ______ 4 ______ 5

______ 6 ______ 7 ______ 8 ______ 9 ______ 10

______ 11 ______ 12 ______ 13 ______ 14 .

Name ______________________ Date __________

Crack the Code

In this puzzle, each letter represents a specific number. Your objective is to place the numbers 0 to 9 in the spaces occupied by the letters of the puzzle. Each letter in the puzzle stands for the same number. When all the letters have been replaced by numbers, you will have decoded the message and the solution should be mathematically correct.

```
       T___ L___ A___
L___ ) E___ Y___ U___
       L___
       T___ Y___
            T___ Y___
            S___ U___
                 U___
                 S___
```

```
     A___ S___
+    A___ S___
     L___ S___
-    T___ S___
     N___ S___
  ×       A___
     Y___ S___
```

```
   Y___ C___ E___
-  E___ L___ T___
   T___ N___ L___
```

```
        P___ P___
+       P___ P___
   T___ P___ U___
```

E___ × E___ = A___ E___

```
        E___ P___ U___
   ×              A___
   T___ T___ P___ Y___
```

```
     A___ L___
  ×       A___
     L___ U___
```

T___ + E___ = Y___ − N___ = N___

E___ + E___ + E___ = T___ E___

0	1	2	3	4	5	6

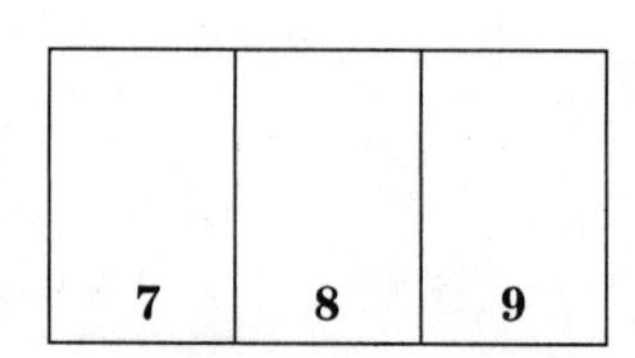

Name ______________________________ Date ____________

Secret Code

In this puzzle, each letter represents a specific number. Your objective is to place the numbers 0 to 9 in the spaces occupied by the letters of the puzzle. Each letter in the puzzle stands for the same number. When all the letters have been replaced by numbers, you will have decoded the message and the solution should be mathematically correct.

```
          S__  M__  U__  E__
     ______________________
W__ ) E__  W__  O__  W__
      S__
      ___
      E__  W__
      E__  W__
      ________
           S__  O__
                W__
           ________
                U__  W__
                U__  W__
                ________
                     S__
```

```
          U__  E__  N__
     __________________
O__ ) A__  E__  W__
      O__
      ___
      P__  E__
      U__  A__
      ________
           W__  W__
           W__  R__
           ________
                U__
```

```
        N__
        A__
        M__
    +   O__
    -------
   E__  S__
```

```
   R__  W__  N__
   ×         N__
   -------------
R__  U__  E__  U__
```

```
     A__  S__
     P__  P__
 +   P__  P__
 ------------
U__  P__  R__
```

```
   O__  M__  P__  A__
 – R__  O__  R__  O__
 --------------------
   P__  S__  A__  P__
```

```
   M__  A__  N__
 – U__  M__  A__
 ---------------
   O__  U__  U__
```

P__ + P__ = P__ × P__

0	1	2	3	4	5	6	7	8	9

Name ______________________ Date ____________

Code-Buster

In this puzzle, each letter represents a specific number. Your objective is to place the numbers 0 to 9 in the spaces occupied by the letters of the puzzle. Each letter in the puzzle stands for the same number. When all the letters have been replaced by numbers, you will have decoded the message and the solution should be mathematically correct.

```
      A__ A__ Y__
E__ ) Y__ I__ L__
      E__
      A__ I__
          E__
          N__ L__
          N__ L__
              W__
```

```
      A__ D__
D__ ) I__ S__
      D__
      A__ S__
      A__ S__
          W__
```

```
      Y__ T__ I__
      I__ L__ S__
   +  Y__ A__ N__
L__ T__ N__ E__
```

```
          Y__ I__ L__
        ×     T__ S__
     I__ N__ A__ L__
L__ E__ I__ S__ W__
T__ D__ L__ N__ L__
```

E__ × L__ = A__ S__ = S__ + A__ W__

```
      Y__ E__
      S__ T__
   +  L__ W__
A__ E__ A__
```

```
     Y__ E__ L__
   - I__ S__ A__
     D__ L__ A__
```

T__ × D__ + W__ − I__ = N__

0	1	2	3	4	5	6	7	8	9

Name ______________________________ Date ______________

Decode My Message

In this puzzle, each letter represents a specific number. Your objective is to place the numbers 0 to 9 in the spaces occupied by the letters of the puzzle. Each letter in the puzzle stands for the same number. When all the letters have been replaced by numbers, you will have decoded the message and the solution should be mathematically correct.

```
        U__ A__
   ×    I__ E__
   ------------
    N__ I__ N__
R__ S__ U__ B__
---------------
A__ A__ T__ N__
```

```
     S__ Q__ A__
+    A__ S__ Q__
----------------
R__ R__ I__ E__
```

```
  A__ A__
  R__ U__
+ B__ E__
---------
  N__ Q__
```

```
  N__ S__
-     E__
---------
  N__ R__
```

```
  E__ U__ T__
- Q__ E__ E__
-------------
  R__ T__ A__
```

R__ × R__ = R__

B__ + B__ = B__ × B__

R__ A__ ÷ U__ = A__

A__ + A__ = A__ × A__

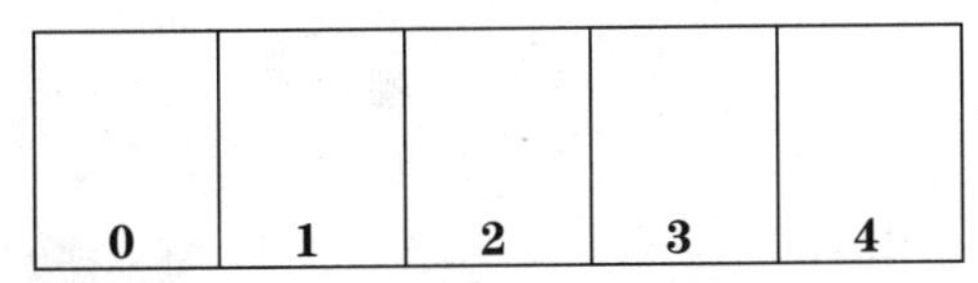

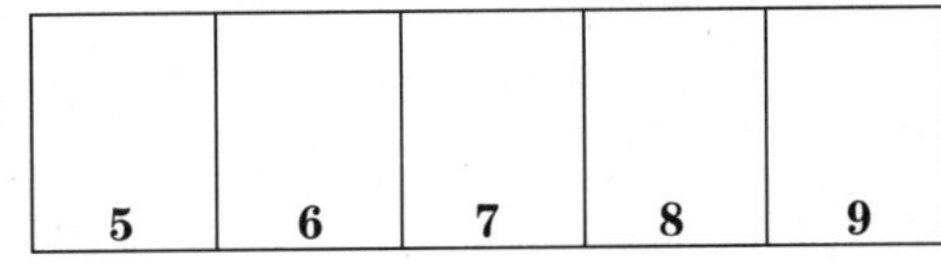

ANSWER KEY

Donut Business (p. 6)

1. + −
2. ÷ +
3. − +
4. + −
5. X −
6. + −
7. − +
8. − −
9. − +
10. − +

Why did the baker stop making donuts?
He was gradually getting very tired of the hole business.

Tic-Tac-Toe (p. 7)

11 O	22 X	15 O
14 X	20 X	17 O
18 X	23 O	21 O

The Zookeeper's Observation (p. 8)

1. + +
2. − −
3. + −
4. − +
5. − X
6. X +
7. + ÷
8. + +
9. X X
10. X ÷

What observation did the zookeeper make about the young kangaroo?
He discovered that it cannot hop and is utterly hopless.

The Dentist's Job (p. 9)

1. 19
2. 5
3. 16
4. 13
5. 7
6. 24
7. 4
8. 10
9. 45
10. 30

How did the dentist describe her work to her friends?
She said it's the same old grind day after day.

Riddle Time (p. 11)

M = 4.18
B = 4.5
W = 3.139
H = .7
N = 6.4
T = .01
A = 9.9
Y = 6.9
C = .3
D = .45
E = .08
R = .002
K = 1.2
I = .07
O = 3.3
S = .9

What happens to people who make sponges?
They become absorbed in their work.

Match It #1 (p. 12)

4.5
1/8
9.1
2/6
8
1 1/4
5 5/12
2.4
3 2/3
3.02
6 4/5

What did the nurse say to the anxious father after his little boy swallowed some coins?
There's no change yet.

Equal Values (p. 13)

22	21	27	144
12	120	40	54
48	29	30	320
300	82	31	60

60 A	54 C	144 A	31 C
48 C	22 A	12 I	320 A
29 C	30 A	82 I	21 C
40 A	27 I	120 C	300 A

What did people say about the girl who couldn't decide if she wanted to be a pilot?
The young girl simply can't make up her mind, she is still up in the air.

Match It #2 (p. 14)

35
95
27
23
222
51
78
12
39
120
36
37
96
29
87
15
19
92
44
48

Where can camels purchase milk?
Dromedairy

Reciprocal Tic-Tac-Toe (p. 15)

Find the reciprocal of: A. 3/30 B. 1/8 10 X 8	Find the reciprocal of: A. 1 1/4 B. 5/9 4/5 O 1 4/5	Find the reciprocal of: A. 5/8 B. 3/4 1 3/5 X 1 1/3
Find the reciprocal of: A. −2/3 B. 5/6 −3/2 O 1 1/5	Find the reciprocal of: A. 1/5 B. 2/6 5 X 3	Find the reciprocal of: A. −4/9 B. 1/2 −9/4 O 2
Find the reciprocal of: A. 1 3/5 B. 2 1/8 3/5 X 8/17	Find the reciprocal of: A. 2/12 B. 2/9 6 O 4 1/2	Find the reciprocal of: A. 5/14 B. 4/8 2 O 2

Let's Play Bingo (p. 16)

1. 5x + 10
2. 6y + 6
3. 5n + 7
4. 7p + 15
5. 7x
6. 5k + 20
7. 2n + 4
8. 14p + 7
9. 9y + 8
10. 7x − 7
11. 8k + 24
12. 4k + 5
13. 7y + 28
14. 5n + 21
15. 10p + 8

Lumberjack Special (p. 17)

8 M 3 P 29 D
17 E 16 H 10 A
81 V

12 I 86 N 7 Y
38 C 2 S 57 L
15 R 44 T 11 O

What specialty food was served at the Lumberjack Café?
They served mainly chops.

Question and Answer (p. 18)

19 7 14 29
13 19 47 8
21 23 79 20
21 3 7 40
27 11 34 53
18 24 79 13

QUESTION: How do most people rate their swimming?
ANSWER: *Most swimmers find that swimming can be easy or hard— it deep-ends.*

The Amazing Waiter (p. 19)

1. $3x - 5$ THE
2. $7x - 9$ WAITER
3. $3x + 3$ WAS
4. x^2 A
5. $7x - 9$ TALENTED
6. $x^2 - 15$ SERVER

What was the tennis-playing waiter's talent?
The waiter was a talented server.

Hidden Answer (p. 20)

I (5, 4); T (-1, -7); S (1, 5); A (-5, -2); N (4, -5); H (2, -2); E (3, 6); I (4, 0); R (-1, 5); R (-7, 6); A (-7, -1); I (-6, 1); S (-1, -1); I (3, -4); N (-5, -6); G (-2, 2); E (-3, 4); X (7, -6); P (2, 1); E (-4, 3); R (-3, -3); I (6, -1); E (0, -5); N (-6, -5); C (7, 3); E (5, -7)

What comment did the parent make about having children?
It's an heir-raising experience.

The Wedding (p. 21)

(3, 1) = C = 6
(-5, -2) = L = 20
(7, -3) = T = 9
(-3, 4) = C = 18
(1, -4) = P = 8
(4, 7) = E = 22
(-4, -7) = R = 4
(-7, 1) = N = 12
(-2, -3) = I = 10
(6, 3) = T = 1
(6, -5) = L = 21
(-2, 2) = A = 14
(5, -2) = E = 16
(-6, -4) = T = 24
(2, 4) = S = 15
(-4, 0) = W = 13
(7, 2) = N = 23
(3, -7) = E = 3
(-5, 6) = O = 11
(2, -1) = H = 2
(-1, 7) = E = 5
(-1, -1) = E = 7
(0, 6) = E = 19
(-3, -5) = X = 17

What did people say after the TV repairman got married?
The reception was excellent.

Movie Star Doctor (p. 22)

1. $2x - 5$ 5
2. $4x + 2$ 30
3. $x + \frac{5}{4}$ 2
4. $x + 8$ 18
5. $x + 15$ 19
6. $8x \div 4$ 6
7. $x - 7$ 3
8. $\frac{1}{2}x$ 4
9. $7x \div 2$ 21
10. $2x + \frac{1}{2}$ $\frac{7}{6} = 1\frac{1}{6}$

Why do lots of movie stars go to the cosmetic surgeon?
The surgeon knows how to raise a few droopy eyebrows.

Hard to Swallow (p. 23)

44 55
81 74
83 51
47 43
46 100
66 64

What happened to the lady who swallowed a spoon?
Within a matter of minutes she quickly learned that she couldn't stir.

Party Animals (p. 24)

PARTY = 2
HIVE = 100
A = 32
THE = 145
HOUSE = 58
HUGE = 11
AT = 41
SWARMING = 45
THEY = 20
HAVE = 47

What do bees do after building a hive?
They have a huge house-swarming party at the hive.

Take Your Pick (p. 27)

KNOW = $7\frac{1}{2}$
TEETH = 8
YOUR = 21
BETTER = $\frac{3}{28}$
YOU = $7\frac{1}{6}$
DO = 7
HAD = 9
IF = 25
THE = 6
REALLY = 15
DIFFERENCE = 13
NOT = $5\frac{1}{3}$
PICK = 12
YOU = 14
NOT = $\frac{1}{10}$

What is the difference between a pitchfork and a toothpick?
If you really do not know the difference you had better not pick your teeth.

Shapely Math (p. 28)

1. 3
2. $2\frac{1}{3}$
3. $5\frac{2}{3}$
4. $3\frac{1}{8}$
5. $2\frac{1}{6}$
6. $4\frac{1}{6}$

Cross Them Out (p. 29)

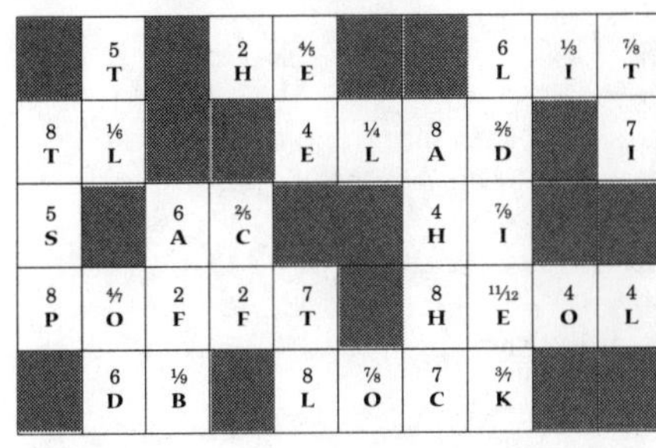

What did people say about the boy who resembled his father, the sculptor?
The little lad is a chip off the old block.

Happiness is . . . ? (p. 30)

2 = THEIR
$2\frac{1}{8}$ = A
$5\frac{1}{4}$ = REALLY
6 = THEY
9 = THEIR
$2\frac{4}{7}$ = OATS
$2\frac{1}{2}$ = MOUTHS
3 = DON'T
7 = IN
5 = WHEN
8 = THEY
$4\frac{2}{7}$ = ENJOY
$1\frac{2}{3}$ = HAVE
$3\frac{1}{3}$ = BIT

When are horses happiest while eating?
They really enjoy their oats when they don't have a bit in their mouths.

Ancient Gatherings (p. 31)

C -6
D 4
Y -8
M 2
E -1
L -2
T -3
F -7
O 0
H 6
E 5
R 1
B -4
P 7
S -5

What did cave dwellers do when they got together?
They formed clubs.

Cats on Vacation (p. 32)

T	O	P	**T**	**H**	I	S	**E**
Y	E	**L**	L	**O**	W	E	R
D	O	**V**	**E**	R	**T**	R	I
H	G	**E**	T	**C**	O	O	L
P	**A**	D	**N**	**A**	T	U	R
E	I	S	**R**	P	**Y**	E	**I**
S	**S**	A	**L**	E	**A**	B	M
S	N	A	**N**	E	**D**	T	**S**

Where do cats like to go on vacation?
They love the Canary Islands.

The Lucky Janitor (p. 33)

10, 4
14 = OFF

0, 5
5 = WITH

-42, -18
-60 = HER

-14, 26
12 = FEET

52, -13
39 = A

-34, -42
-76 = SWEPT

-8, -50
-58 = BROOM

25, -40
-15 = HER

How did the janitor meet his wife?
He . . . swept her off her feet with a broom.

Let's Play Ball (p. 34)

7 = HOME
13 = GET
8 = PLATE
12 = TO
3 = HE
9 = HE
6 = TO
14 = WALKED
5 = UP
4 = GOT
11 = SURE
2 = WHENEVER
10 = WAS

Why did the toy poodle like to play base-ball?
Whenever he got up to home plate he was sure to get walked.

The Noisy Twins (p. 35)

HE = 162
REFERRED = 160
TO = 153
THE = 144
IDENTICAL = 114
TWIN = 112
BOYS = 100
AS = 50
STEREO = 5
SPEAKERS = 4

What did the man say about the pair of loud twins?
He referred to the identical twin boys as stereo speakers.

The Lost Timepiece (p. 36)

$E = \sqrt{81}$
$A = 3^4$
$T = \sqrt{121}$
$S = \sqrt{100}$
$U = 6^2$
$Y = \sqrt{25}$
$L = 5^3$
$C = \sqrt{144}$
$M = 2^5$
$H = \sqrt{64}$
$B = 4^3$
$I = 3^3$

What happened to the beautiful lady who lost her watch?
She became a timeless beauty.

The Young Artist (p. 37)

TRUE	TRUE
FALSE	FALSE
FALSE	FALSE
TRUE	FALSE
FALSE	TRUE
FALSE	FALSE
FALSE	FALSE
FALSE	TRUE
TRUE	

Why couldn't the young artist draw a cube?
The artists just couldn't—due to a mental block.

The Clockmakers' Cat (p. 38)

{0, 1, 2, 3, 4, 5}	{5, 6, 7, 8 . . .}	{0, 1, 2, 3, 4, 5, 6}
{7, 8, 9, 10 . . .}	{0, 1}	{4, 5, 6, 7, 8}
{0, 1, 2, 3}	{0, 1, 2, 3, 4}	{3, 4, 5, 6 . . .}
{4, 5, 6, 7, 8 . . .}	{0, 1, 2, 3, 4, 5, 6, 7, 8}	{2, 3, 4, 5 . . .}

What did the clockmakers find out about their cat?
When they took it to the veterinarian's they discovered it had ticks.

The Unhappy Tree (p. 39)

(30, 9) P 5	(82, 55) L 1
(54, 2916) E 9	(21, 16) U 7
(12, 144) C 8	(27, 160) U 2
(36, 81) R 6	(17, 65) S 4
(16, 13) B 0	(9, 99) E 3

Which evergreen tree always seems unhappy?
The blue spruce.

The Curious Boy (p. 40)

399996
THE (12)
3999996
CURIOUS (5)
4900
WANTED (9)
8100
WAS (3)
44442222
BUTTER (13)
444444222222
SEE (11)
6.36363
AND (6)
3.63636
BOY (2)
123454321
SIMPLY (8)
1234567654321
TO (10)
1599
THE (1)
3599
FLY (14)
244442
VERY (4)
24444442
HE (7)

Why did the little boy throw the butter off the balcony?
The boy was very curious and he simply wanted to see the butter fly.

Crack the Code (p. 42)

STANLEY CUP

Secret Code (p. 43)

SUPERWOMAN

Code Buster (p. 44)

WALT DISNEY

Decode My Message (p. 45)

BRAIN QUEST